THE GOLDEN AGE OF ROMAN LITERATURE

Ancient History Picture Books
Children's Ancient History

BABY PROFESSOR
EDUCATION KIDS

Speedy Publishing LLC

40 E. Main St. #1156

Newark, DE 19711

www.speedypublishing.com

Copyright 2017

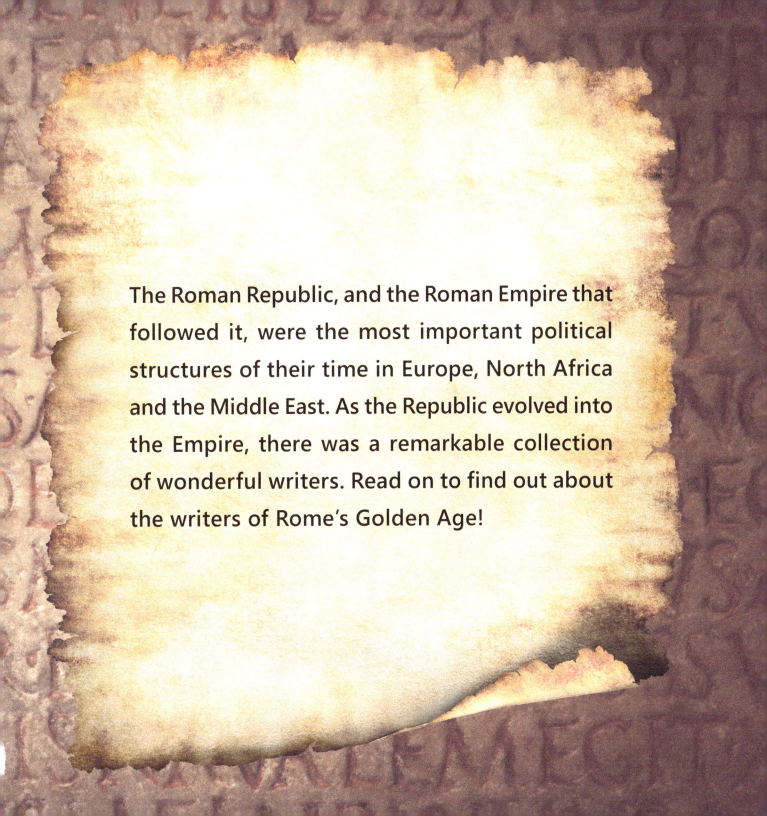

The Roman Republic, and the Roman Empire that followed it, were the most important political structures of their time in Europe, North Africa and the Middle East. As the Republic evolved into the Empire, there was a remarkable collection of wonderful writers. Read on to find out about the writers of Rome's Golden Age!

REPUBLIC BECOMES EMPIRE

Rome rose over the centuries from being a single small community on the edge of the Tiber River in Italy, to controlling territory all around the Mediterranean Sea. It went as far north as Scotland, and as far east as what is now Persia. Rome's armies were better trained and usually had better generals than the armies they faced, and gradually the Republic expanded. Read the Baby Professor book The Battles of Rome to learn more about what the Roman army did.

In the second century BC, Rome defeated its great rival Carthage in North Africa, and its rival Corinth in Greece. This brought in a period of relative peace and prosperity. More Romans had time for art, writing, philosophy and other non-military pursuits. In the arts, there was a movement toward writing for pleasure and self-expression: "art for art's sake".

At the same time, however, pressure was still growing on the Republic. There were challenges from the east and north. Strong leaders inside the Republic felt the government was too slow and too weak to control Rome's huge territory well. As Rome moved into a struggle over who would lead it, writers enlisted on various sides to argue for the Republic, for a king, or for some other sort of strong leader.

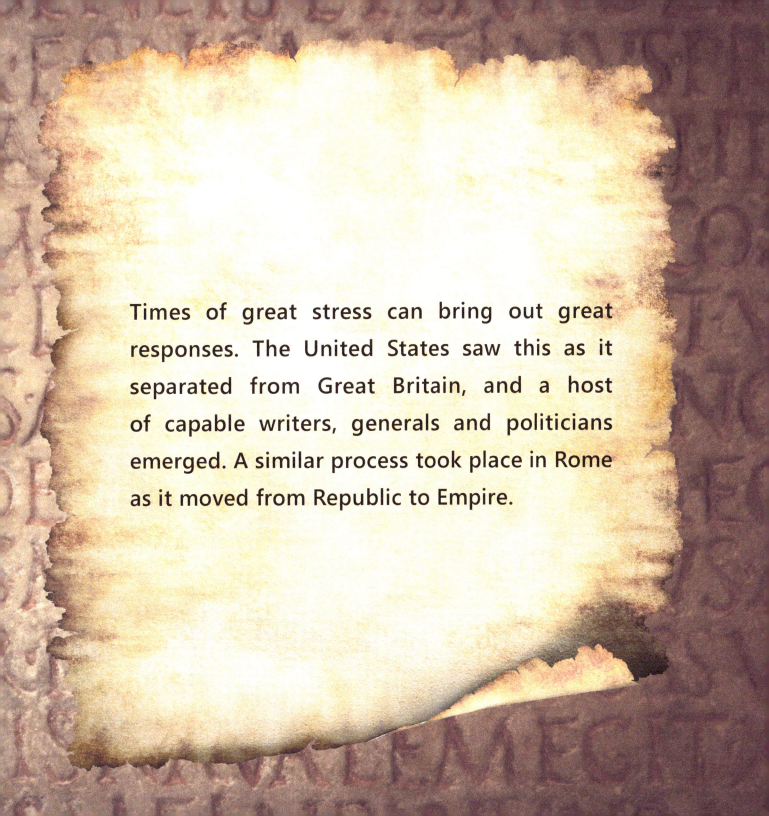

Times of great stress can bring out great responses. The United States saw this as it separated from Great Britain, and a host of capable writers, generals and politicians emerged. A similar process took place in Rome as it moved from Republic to Empire.

THE WAY ROMANS WROTE

In both the Republic and the Empire, Roman writers generally used Latin for important material. However, most educated Romans also knew and could write Greek. This was useful for writing to people in the eastern part of the Empire, where Greek was the everyday language.

ΠΙϹΤΕΥΩ ΕΙϹ ΕΝΑ ΘΟΝ, ΠΑΤΕΡΑ ΠΑΝΤΟΚΡΑΤΟΡΑ, ΠΟΙΗΤΗΝ ΟΥΡΑΝΟΥ Κ ΓΗϹ
ΟΡΑΤΩΝ ΤΕ ΠΑΝΤΩΝ Κ ΑΟΡΑΤΩΝ. ΚΕΙϹ ΕΝΑ ΚΝ ΙΗϹΟΥΝ ΧΝ ΤΝ ΥΙΟΝ
ΤΥ ΘΥ ΤΟΝ ΜΝΟΓΕΝΗ, ΤΝ ΕΚ ΤΟ ΠΡΟϹ ΓΕΝΝΗΘΕΝΤΑ ΠΡ ΠΑΝΤΩΝ ΤΩΝ ΑΙΩΝΩ
ΦΩϹ ΕΚ ΦΩΤΟϹ ΘΕΟΝ ΑΛΗΘΙΝΟΝ ΕΚ ΘΕΥ ΑΛΘΙΝΥ ΓΕΝΝΘΕΝΤΑ, Υ
ΠΟΙΗΘΕΝΤΑ, ΟΜΟΟΥϹΙΟΝ ΤΩ ΠΡΙ ΔΙ Υ ΤΑ ΠΑΝΤΑ ΕΓΕΝΤΟ Ο ΔΙ ΗΜΑϹ ΤΟϹ
ΑΝΘΡΩΠΥϹ Κ ΔΑ ΤΗΝ ΗΜΕΤΕΡΑΝ ϹΩΤΗΡΙΑΝ ΚΑΤΕΛΘΟΝΤΑ ΕΚ ΤΩ ΟΥΡΑΝΩ
Κ ϹΑΡΚΩΘΕΝΤΑ ΕΚ ΠΝΕΥΜΑΤΟϹ ΑΓΙΥ Κ ΜΡΙΑϹ ΤΗϹ ΠΑΡΘΕΝΥ Κ ΕΝΑΝΘ
ΡΗϹΑΝΤΑ. ϹΤΑΥΡΩΘΕΝΤΑ ΤΕ ΥΠΡ ΗΜΩ ΕΠΙ ΠΟΝΤΙΥ ΠΙΛΑΤΟΥ
ΚΑΙ ΠΑΘΟΝΤΑ, ΚΑΙ ΤΑΦΕΝΤΑ...

Virgil

It was also useful for studying the great Greek literature that Romans considered part of their heritage. Roman plays, poems, histories, and philosophical works draw heavily on the examples of the Greeks who wrote before them. For example, when Virgil wrote the great Latin epic poem, the Aeneid, he drew heavily on Homer's Iliad for both style and subject matter.

Romans wrote important documents on scrolls made of papyrus (a plant that grows in Egypt) or from animal skins. They dipped a metal pin in ink and used that to write with. For day-to-day writing they used wax tablets they could smooth out and re-use, or wrote with charcoal or ink on thin pieces of wood. In the far edge of the Empire, at Hadrian's Wall between what is now England and Scotland, researchers have found a huge collection of notes, letters, and other documents written on pieces of wood about the size of postcards.

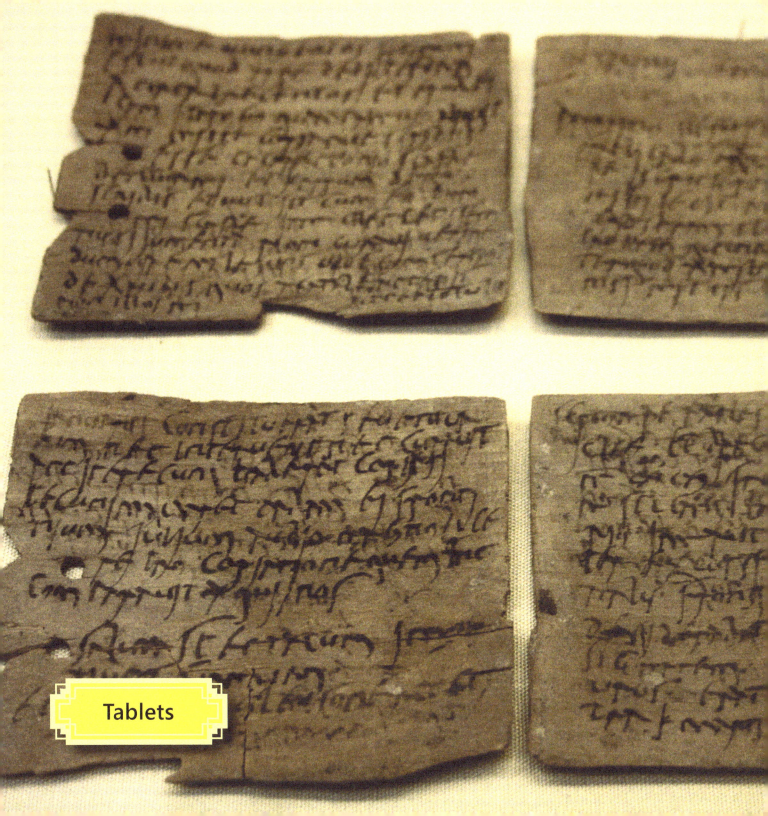

Tablets

There were no printing presses, so the only way to "publish" a book was to have slaves or hired copyists make many, many copies of it. After the Roman Empire fell, all copies of many important works were destroyed or lost. That is why, for many great writers, we know the titles of a lot of books that they wrote, but not what was in them.

THE TWO GOLDEN AGES

The Golden Age of Roman literature spans the end of the Roman Republic and its evolution into the Roman Empire. It runs from about 70 BCE to about 18 CE, less than a hundred years.

TIITYRETVPATVLERECVBANSSVBTEGMINEFAGI
SILVESTREMTENVIMVSAMMEDITARISAVENA
NOSPATRIAEFINISETDVLCIALINQVIMVSARVA
NOSPATRIAMFVGIMVSTVTITYRELENTVSINVMBRA
FORMOSAMRESONAREDOCESAMARYLLIDASILVAS
OMELIBOEEDEVSNOBISHAECOTIAFECIT
NAMQVEERITILLEMIHISEMPERDEVSILLIVSARAM
SAEPETENERNOSTRISABOVILIBVSIMBVETAGNVS
ILLEMEASERRAREBOVESVTCERNISETIPSVM

Historians divide the Golden Age into an earlier and later period: the Age of Cicero and the Augustan Age.

The Age of Cicero

The Age of Cicero, from about 70 to 42 BCE, is named after the greatest writer of this time, but there were many other prominent writers as well.

Cicero

Julius Caesar

The writers of this period were men of action as well as story-tellers and historians. Several served as generals in the civil war between Julius Caesar and Pompey, and others were politicians, scientific farmers and students of nature.

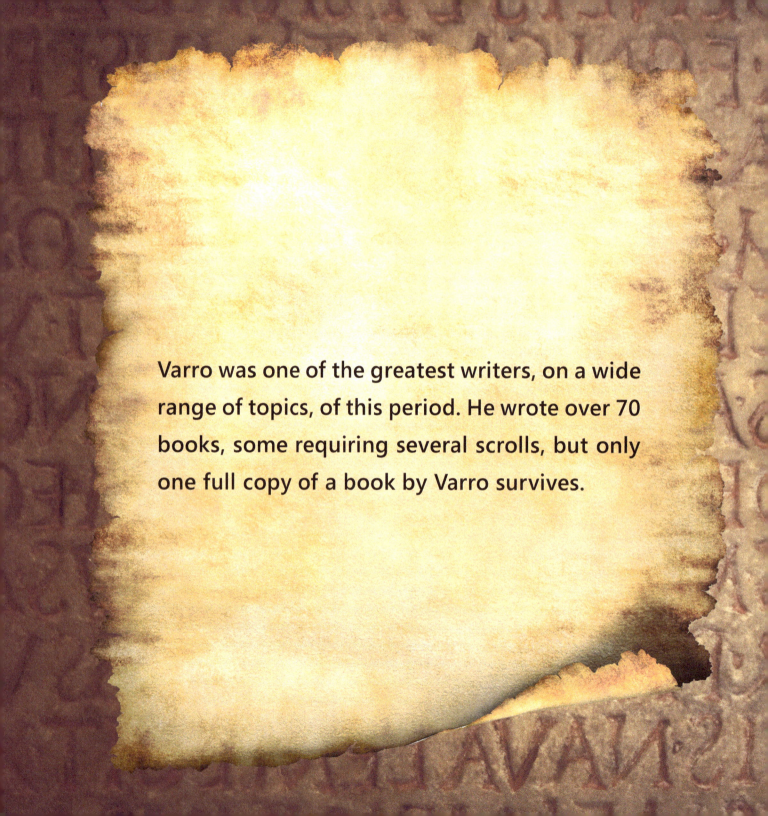

Varro was one of the greatest writers, on a wide range of topics, of this period. He wrote over 70 books, some requiring several scrolls, but only one full copy of a book by Varro survives.

Varro

Mark Antony

Varro led an army against Julius Caesar during Caesar's struggle with Pompey. After Caesar won, he pardoned Varro; but Mark Antony exiled Varro from Rome after Caesar's murder. Many years later Augustus, the first emperor of Rome, let Varro return home.

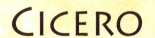Cicero

Cicero was a senator and a powerful politician. As a writer, he developed and modelled a style of writing that tried to express clearly abstract concepts like honor, patriotism and pride. His prose style was so influential that most later writers either imitated him or set out to write in a way that was as far from Cicero's style as was possible.

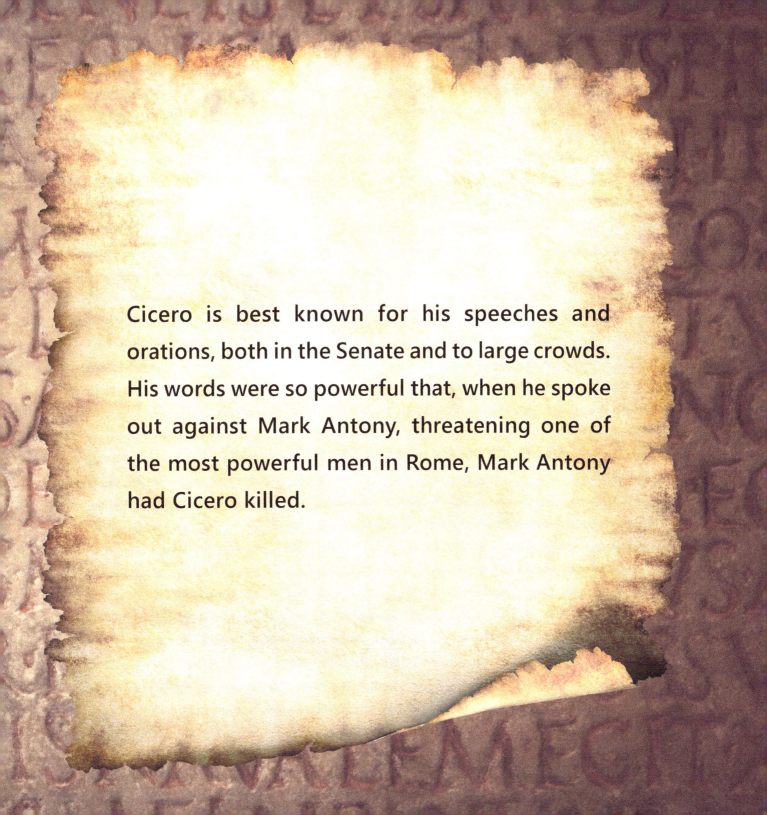

Cicero is best known for his speeches and orations, both in the Senate and to large crowds. His words were so powerful that, when he spoke out against Mark Antony, threatening one of the most powerful men in Rome, Mark Antony had Cicero killed.

Virgil

Virgil was born near Mantua and grew up near Milan. He tried to create flowing, graceful prose in the style of classical Greek writing.

Virgil wrote The Aeneid, which is to Romans what The Iliad and The Odyssey are to Greeks. It starts with the fall of Troy at the end of the Trojan war, and follows Prince Aeneas and his people as they journey to Italy and found what will be Rome. The whole epic is an explanation of why it is good and natural for Rome to conquer other peoples.

HORACE

Horace was another general on the losing side in the war between Caesar and Pompey. When not serving in the army, he wrote light and sometimes amusing verses on serious topics. His flowing, rhyming lines are a type of "lyric poetry", like the words to a song. Because he reveals so much about himself in his verse, some say Horace wrote the world's first autobiography.

Julius Caesar

Julius Caesar

Julius Caesar was a general, a statesman, and a nation builder. He rose to fame partly by conquering Gaul, what is now France, and partly because he wrote a book about the campaigns in Gaul that became very popular. Caesar wrote in a very clear and simple style that makes his descriptions easy to follow. When United States President Ulysses S. Grant wrote about his time as a general during the U.S. Civil War, he took Caesar's writing style as his example.

THE AUGUSTAN AGE

Octavian, the adopted son of Julius Caesar, eventually won the long war for power in Rome and became its ruler under the name Augustus. Augustus encouraged writers not to try to say new things in new ways, but rather to try to say old things better.

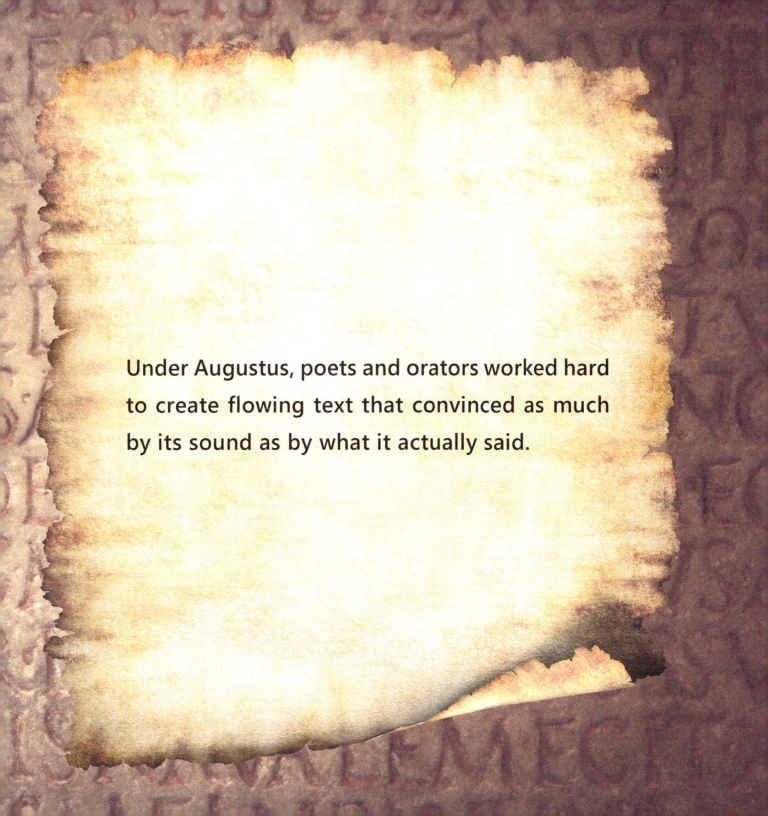

Under Augustus, poets and orators worked hard to create flowing text that convinced as much by its sound as by what it actually said.

Another aspect of the Augustan age was that the emperor did not enjoy criticism or writings that did not agree with what the government wanted published. A writer who published something judged unacceptable might find himself imprisoned, exiled or even executed. As you can expect, a lot of the writing of this age says very nice things about the emperor and the government!

Virgil and Horace continued writing under Augustus, and new authors rose up as well. They included:

PROPERTIUS

We do not know much about Propertius beyond the skill of his poetry. He is best known for four books of love poems addressed to a woman he calls "Cynthia".

Propertius and Cynthia

Ovid

OVID

Ovid was also famous for his love poems, but his most famous work is an epic, Metamorphoses. The epic is the history of the whole world from its creation to when Julius Caesar, the emperor's adopted father, dies and is made into a God. This was very popular with the emperor's supporters!

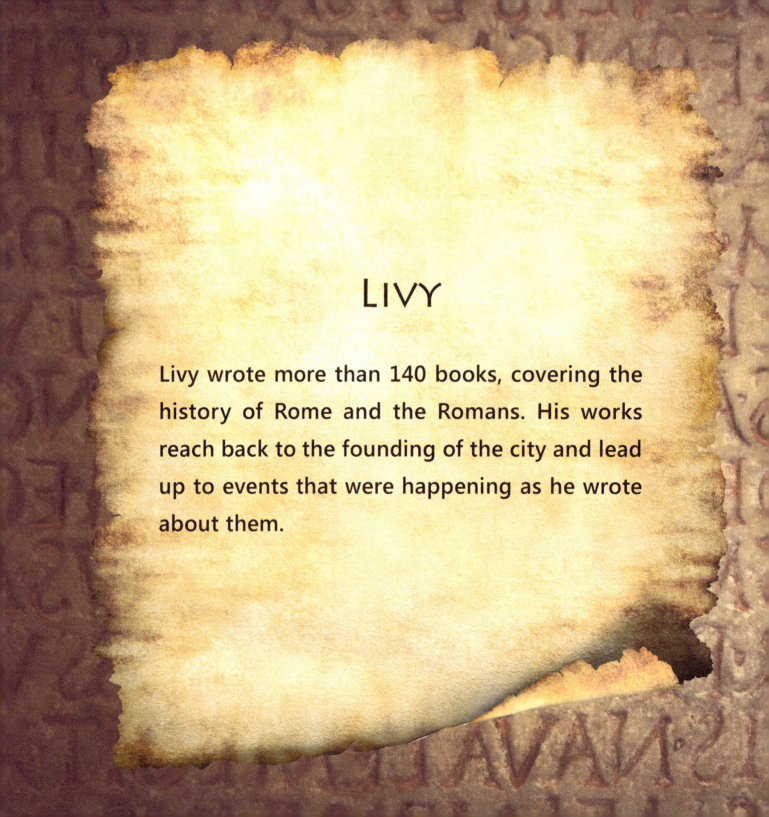

LIVY

Livy wrote more than 140 books, covering the history of Rome and the Romans. His works reach back to the founding of the city and lead up to events that were happening as he wrote about them.

Pliny the Elder

Pliny the Elder was a general and admiral, a student of natural history, and a prolific writer. He wrote manuals on public speaking, instructions on how to throw a spear while riding a horse, and over 30 books on the natural world. He died while trying to study, and to rescue people from, the eruption of Mount Vesuvius.

WRITERS CELEBRATE THE WORLD

From the invention of writing right up to today, writers look at the world and then write down what they see and think about it. This helps us understand the world better. Read other Baby Professor books, like Get Involved! Famous People during the French Revolution, Who Was Joseph Stalin? and Archimedes and his Numbers, to learn how other great people in the past helped create the world we live in today.

Visit

BABY PROFESSOR
EDUCATION KIDS

www.BabyProfessorBooks.com

to download Free Baby Professor eBooks
and view our catalog of new and exciting
Children's Books

CPSIA information can be obtained
at www.ICGtesting.com
Printed in the USA
BVHW012255130222
628923BV00022BA/415